LINKEDIN SALES

MACHINE:

THE SECRET STRATEGY TO GENERATE LEADS AND SALES ON LINKEDIN - IN 30 MINUTES/DAY

By
Raza Imam

www.JaggedEdgeDigital.com

TABLE OF CONTENTS

Free Training Video

Thank you for buying LinkedIn Sales Machine. If you follow the advice in this book, you'll get amazing results.

If you want a free training webinar that walks you through the entire process, provides live examples, and shares real-life results, then go to:

www.JaggedEdgeDigital.com/LinkedInRiches

It's a brief webinar by my friend and mentor John Nemo that walks through the entire process of marketing on LinkedIn. I've watched it multiple times and learned a ton from it.

More Help

If you're interested in:

- More advice

- A done-for-you marketing service

- Training for you and your team

email me at raza.imam@jaggededgedigital.com to discuss how we can work together.

SHORT AND SWEET (BECAUSE WE'RE ALL BUSY)

"Give me a one-page bullet-list of exactly what I should do. That's worth more to me than a stack of books that I have to dig through to get to the good stuff. I may give you 50 bucks for the books. But I'll pay you $5,000 for the one page."

-Alwyn Cosgrove, fitness coach, trainer, entrepreneur

You're busy.

I'm busy.

We're all busy.

It's an epidemic of the modern age.

That's why I kept this book short and sweet.

It's practical, it's tactical, and it's actionable.

Why?

2

Because I want to give you the meat and potatoes so that you can get started and take things to the next level - as soon as possible.

Because if you're like me, time is your most valuable asset.

Honestly, who actually has time to read 200-300 page books? With 3 young kids that need my attention, I sure don't!

It's also why CEO's have executive summaries prepared for them. Rather than spending hours and hours pouring over detailed reports, they need the most valuable information, distilled into actionable insights, so that they can make critical decisions and take action.

That's what I want for you.

You'll notice that there's a lot that I ***don't*** talk about in this book; that's for a reason.

I don't want to teach you about starting a group, or the intricate details of LinkedIn Sales Navigator, or how to make posts go viral, or how to get higher video engagement, or how to get tens of thousands of connections and followers.

There are other, more comprehensive manuals on LinkedIn that will teach you all of that.

My goal is to give you the quickest, easiest, simplest way to find leads and make sales on LinkedIn, not to make you a viral LinkedIn celebrity.

While that stuff is really cool, I don't know how much revenue it translates to.

Please note, I write in short, punchy paragraphs that are usually one or two sentences long. I do this because it makes it much easier for me to crank out ideas. When I write, I write from the heart and writing short paragraphs like this is a part of that.

I hope you enjoy reading this book as much as I enjoyed writing it.

SOME STRAIGHT TALK ON LINKEDIN

"LinkedIn is USELESS and a colossal waste of time."

That's what used to think 6 months ago.

Until two clients contacted me and paid me over $20,000.

Out of the blue.

They found me on LinkedIn.

One was someone that I'd known for a while. I had offered services to him in the past but he didn't need them. Then he saw one of my posts on LinkedIn and contacted me.

Another one found me out of the blue. He did a LinkedIn search for "online marketing", saw my profile, contacted me, and ended up hiring me.

"Amazing" I thought to myself.

Then I spoke to a guy that earned $130k for his consulting business in 90 days.

All from LinkedIn.

"Hmm, maybe I should be taking LinkedIn more seriously" I thought.

Then I spoke to another guy that makes $50k on LinkedIn for his business.

"Wow, this isn't just a one-off thing" I thought.

Then a friend told me he was recruited for a job at JP Morgan Chase - out of the blue.

From - you guessed it -LinkedIn.

"That's it, I'm going to buckle down and figure LinkedIn out"

There are no tricks.

No shortcuts.

No secrets.

All it takes is a well-optimized profile like I teach later in this book.

And creating intimacy with your audience, which I reveal later in the book as well.

If you're a storyteller and like creating content, you can do that also - but it's not necessary (or even all that profitable)

The key is to focus on a particular audience, work relentlessly to solve their problems, and do it in a helpful, professional, non-salesly way.

If you can do that, then there's a world of opportunity on LinkedIn.

You just have to know how to tap into it.

Interested?

You should be.

WHO THIS BOOK IS FOR

Is this book for you?

Well, let me ask you a few questions.

Are you a coach, consultant, freelancer, recruiter, CEO, lawyer, financial advisor, speaker, author, marketer, founder, salesperson, journalist, investor, or trainer - just to name a few?

If so, this book is for you.

Do you offer a business to business service, or offer a service for professionals?

If so, this book is for you.

Are you responsible for driving business, generating leads, closing sales, building relationships, or growing your reach?

If so, this book is for you.

Don't get me wrong, anyone can use LinkedIn to grow their career, but this book is meant for entrepreneurs, or anyone with the responsibility to grow a business and generate leads and sales.

So assuming that you can benefit from this book, I've got a difficult question to ask. You don't have to answer me, but I do want you to honestly answer yourself.

It's a question that I ask of myself also. And sometimes the answer isn't pretty. But when I own up to it, I'm able to focus on what I need to do to make things better.

So here's the question...

How's *YOUR* business doing?

Are you generating as much revenue as you think you could?

Are you consistently getting qualified leads speaking to you day in, day out?

Do you feel like you're constantly scrambling trying to make ends meet? Hunting for leads, dealing with gatekeepers, facing rejection after rejection?

That's the thing about business; you can have the best offering in the world, but if you can't find your ideal prospects consistently, you don't have a business.

Leads and sales are the lifeblood of your business, so it's crucial to have a system to constantly fill your pipeline.

And if you have a B2B offering or help professionals, LinkedIn is one of the best ways to do it.

I know a guy that sells online courses and he does quite well prospecting on LinkedIn.

I know of a guy that offers copywriting services, and he gets almost all of his leads on LinkedIn.

I know of another guy that offers digital marketing services, and he gets almost all of his business from LinkedIn.

I know another guy that offers business strategy services, and you guessed it, he gets almost all of his leads from LinkedIn.

And I want the same for you.

But, you have to commit to it and you have to provide value.

That means pulling out all the stops, getting creative, and thinking outside of the box. It also means investing time and energy in learning the process.

You also have to be great at what you do. That means you have to be results-oriented and obsessively focused on doing what's best for your clients.

Your solution has to solve their problem, better, faster, cheaper, or more elegantly than your competitors. It has to add value to their lives. It has to deliver measurable results.

Preferably all of the above.

If you can do that, then you're virtually guaranteed to have a growing, thriving, wildly successful business. Because at the end of the day, everyone wants results.

Lastly, you have to know your numbers. This is a tough one for me because I'm an "idea" guy. I'm a marketer. I love growing my business. Tracking the numbers and staying focused on my income and expenses is something I could stand to do better with.

So whether you're a numbers person, or whether you delegate that to someone else, you have to be obsessively focused on what's working. You want to use data to make decisions that turn into revenue.

THE 6 BIGGEST MISTAKES KEEPING YOU FROM GENERATING BUSINESS FROM LINKEDIN

Mistake.1: You're Focused on Selling

I can almost hear you asking yourself:

"Wait, isn't this book called LinkedIn Sales Machine?"

Yes, this book is called "LinkedIn Sales Machine", but LinkedIn is NOT a sales platform.

Sure, the end goal is to make a sale and grow your business, but that's not the first step - not by a long shot.

Please keep that firmly in mind.

Though it's not a sales platform, it **IS** a relationship building platform. It's a place to find your ideal clients, it's a place to learn about them, it's a place to create a relationship. It's a place to showcase how you can solve their problem.

Don't worry, because later in this book, I'm going to show you exactly how to do that.

Mistake.2: You're Not Working Outside of LinkedIn

Yes, LinkedIn is a fantastic way to find and connect with people.

But if you focus exclusively on LinkedIn, you'll be disappointed with the results.

That's because LinkedIn, as powerful as it is, can be a bit clunky. And people aren't on LinkedIn as obsessively as they are on Facebook, Twitter, and Instagram.

LinkedIn is an awesome place to get information about people, but remember, you also have email, their company blog, and Twitter at your disposal.

Don't worry though, because I show you how to use all of these tools to get on your prospects radar later in this book.

Mistake.3: You Aren't Investing Time on LinkedIn

Some of the most successful people on LinkedIn are absolutely committed to it.

They invest time.

They create systems.

They have a process.

They are consistent.

Some people use tools that automate outreach and messaging on LinkedIn.

Some people spend an hour a day prospecting on LinkedIn. Some people dedicate a few hours, twice a week to build relationships on LinkedIn.

Regardless of the strategy they use, they're serious about LinkedIn - and that's why they get results.

Mistake.4: You Aren't Creating Content

You may have a lot of connections on LinkedIn, but how engaged are they with you?

Sure, LinkedIn will send them a message if you get a new job, or if you have a birthday.

But how well do they know what you're working on?

Do they understand the problems you solve?

Do they know how you can help them?

If not, it's probably because you aren't creating content on LinkedIn. From posts, to articles, to videos, there are plenty of great ways to get the interest of your existing connections.

In fact, I used this technique to get a $20,000 contract from an existing connection of mine.

Don't worry, I'll show you how I did it.

Mistake.5: You Aren't Talking About Their Problems

The easiest way to get people's attention is to talk about them. Think about it. If you walk into a party and start talking about *your* outfit, how many conversations do you think you'll have?

But what if you walk up to a stranger and talk about *their* outfit, *their* glasses, *their* shoes?

16

In a business sense, you take it one step further by talking about their **problems**.

Then you can bridge that to how you figured out a way to help them.

Think of it like this, if you get together at the park and meet with a bunch of local moms, it's easy to talk about how hard it is to get your kids to go to sleep. Or the challenges you're having potty training your kids. Or how one of your kids has social anxiety. Or the struggles of having teenage drivers.

By simply talking about their problems, you're building empathy with them.

Now imagine if you had a solution to any of these problems? What if you were able to share how you solved the problem for yourself and others?

That's what you want to do on LinkedIn.

I hope you're seeing the power of talking about other people's problems.

On LinkedIn, you want to do that via creating content in the form of posts, articles, and videos that I mentioned above.

17

Mistake.6: You Don't Have a Transformational Product or Service

Lastly, people don't care about you, your company, your software, your consulting, your investment opportunity, or anything else about you.

What they **_do_** care about is themselves.

So you have to position your product or service to help **_them_**. It has to solve a problem and promise a transformation.

I once read an article about a guy that paid $1,300 for an office chair.

At first he thought that was a ridiculous price to pay, given the fact that he could easily buy one for $100.

But he said he eventually bought that $1,300 office chair because he works at a desk all day and it was the solution to his years of agonizing back pain.

The company didn't sell him a chair, they sold him a solution to his debilitating back pain.

And he eagerly bought it.

That's powerful stuff.

I want you to employ the same thought process.

Think in terms of how your product or service will transform your prospects life.

WHY LINKEDIN?

Like I said in the previous chapter, LinkedIn is a virtual goldmine for B2B companies.

If you offer products or services to other businesses, or if you offer a product or service to professionals, you want to be on LinkedIn.

But I wasn't always convinced of that. Like I mentioned earlier, I thought LinkedIn was a waste of time. That was until I was exposed to how people are actually using LinkedIn.

The statistics are ***staggering***.

At the time of this writing, LinkedIn has 500 million users.

From Fortune 500 CEO's, to Silicon Valley entrepreneurs, to doctors, lawyers, VP's, directors, managers, investors, and everything in between.

Most of them are actively engaged on LinkedIn, or at least pay attention and take it seriously.

Of those 500 million users, nearly 250 million log in each month, making for a pretty active user base.

Of those 250 million active users, up to 40% of them log in daily. And with their mobile app, there are an estimated 60+ million mobile users of LinkedIn.

Of all these users, an estimated 61 million are senior level influencers and 40 million are in decision making positions.

So LinkedIn has garnered an incredibly successful, incredibly influential user base that actively logs onto the site.

LinkedIn is so valuable in fact, that Microsoft paid over $26 billion to buy the company back in 2016.

And you better believe that LinkedIn is doing everything they can to increase those numbers. In fact, their CEO, Jeff Weiner even said that he wants LinkedIn to be the home of all working professionals across the world.

So expect to see continued growth on LinkedIn.

For all of these reasons, LinkedIn is truly a B2B business person's dream come true.

Think about it, a platform with over 500 million users (and growing), most of which have detailed information like job title, industry, experience, schools, groups and clubs, and even hobbies - all on the platform expecting to be approached by like-minded business people.

It's unheard of.

Now if you play your cards right, if you're professional and tactful, if you focus on providing value and building a relationship, you can reach out to these people, connect with them, and do business together.

It's a beautiful thing.

No wonder LinkedIn marketing is red hot right now.

But there's a right way to do it, and a wrong way to do it.

As a B2B company, it's incredibly important that you use LinkedIn correctly. If not, you're leaving money on the table. And if you do it wrong, you'll end up burning bridges, destroying your reputation, and leaving a bad taste in people's mouth.

But don't worry, because that's what I'm going to reveal to you in this book.

You'll discover the simple strategy you can use to find highly qualified leads, and turn them into connections that look forward to working with you.

So no matter what stage your business is at, NOW is the best time to get started with marketing on LinkedIn.

Because most of your competitors are doing it wrong.

They're spamming their prospects. They're talking about themselves. They're trying to be everything to everybody.

Kind of like that annoying guy at a party that schmoozes everyone handing out business cards.

The simple strategy I teach in this book will make you stand out because you'll be focusing on your prospect. But I'll get to that later in this book.

For now, I want you to think about the opportunity on LinkedIn, to get excited, to feel the power that you have at the tip of your fingertips.

Just imagine how much revenue you could earn in the next 90 days if you use these strategies correctly. How would that change your business? Your life?

And believe me, it's possible to radically transform your business, whether your goal is to get from $100k in revenue to $200k, or $250k in revenue to $500k/year. Or higher.

I know this is a bold claim, but other people and companies are doing this all day long. Of course, you have to have a good product or service, and you have to be selling it at a premium price.

Consider the fact that at any given point in time, roughly 3% of the market is ready to buy from you. You just have to be there at the right time.

The hard part is actually sifting through tons of leads to find those high probability prospects.

One of my mentors once said it's like sifting through a deck of cards, looking for the aces. You don't want to jam a square peg in a round hole. You don't want to "force", or "convince", or "persuade" people into buying what you have. That's way too hard and emotionally draining.

Instead, you want to search, sort, sift, and filter through prospects to find those diamonds. The companies that are primed to buy from you, that have a problem you can solve, and that are motivated to take action.

If you view it that way, selling becomes a lot more fun. A game of sorts where you're looking for your ideal client. Starting a conversation with them, and ultimately discussing their problem so accurately, so acutely, with such precision, that they can't help but pay you to solve it.

In other words, how likely are they to buy from you? Do they have the kinds of problems that you know how to solve? Are they motivated to solve them? How much is their problem costing them? What are the consequences of not working with you?

Those are the questions you have to answer before you start LinkedIn outreach.

Because the more specific and targeted your answers are, the better results you're going to get.

That makes the tedious, boring, draining process of prospecting so much more fun and easy.

Sample Outreach Numbers

Now, you just have to work backward and calculate how many conversations you need to have to close one client.

Then calculate how many outreach messages do you need to have one conversation.

Simple.

So let's say you contact 100 companies per month on LinkedIn. That's about 25 per week, or 5 per day.

Out of those 100 companies you've contacted, let's say that 20 respond to you (1 per day) That's a 20% conversion rate.

Let's say those turn into real live phone calls, or sales presentations, or in-person meetings.

And out of those 20 conversations let's say only 2 buy from you (I know that's abysmally low, but let's be ultra-conservative with our estimates here), that's a 2% overall conversion rate.

Now if you sell a high-ticket product or service, like a SaaS product, or consulting, or industrial equipment, or executive coaching, or training that could translate into a hefty chunk of change.

For most businesses, closing 2 to 4 high-ticket sales per month would be an absolute game changer.

And with LinkedIn, it's a lot more attainable than you might think.

So the secret to making more sales is having more conversations with qualified decision makers in your target market. And if you have a B2B offering, the #1 place to be is on LinkedIn.

To prove my point, just imagine filling your calendar with 1-5 super qualified leads per day. Imagine having conversations with people that are actually excited to speak to you. Imagine offering your products and services to people that are looking for exactly what you have.

Yes it takes planning, it takes work, it takes a well-executed system, *but it's completely possible.*

And if you're willing to invest just one hour per day, it's completely worth it.

Action Item:

So right now, this very instant I want you to commit that you're going to take action.

I want you to commit that you're going to do what it takes to figure out how to use LinkedIn properly.

I want you to commit that you're going to implement what I teach you, and invest an hour a day actually going through the process.

Because trust me, there's nothing like having intelligent, motivated, high-quality prospects responding to you on LinkedIn.

So are you with me?

Good.

I can't wait to get share these tips with you.

THE 1 SECRET TO SUCCESS ON LINKEDIN

So here's a topic that weighs heavily on me. If you get this right, getting business on LinkedIn will be ten times easier.

In fact, getting clients, partners, and even rockstar employees will be ten times easier - not just on LinkedIn, but in life.

What's the secret?

Well, Zig Ziglar said it best when he said:

"You can get everything in life you want if you will just help enough other people get what they want."

So that means that you have to focus every single thing that you do on LinkedIn around your ideal client. Focus on your prospect... everything should be about THEM.

The beauty is the LinkedIn gives you so many opportunities to demonstrate how you help them.

Here are a few examples:

- **Your Profile**: Your profile should be focused on your prospect. That means it should **not** read like a resume. It should not list your accomplishments. Instead, it should focus on what you can do for them. It should focus on the problems you solve. It should focus on the results you deliver and the audience that you help.

- **Your Headline**: Your headline should be clear, direct, and compelling. It should talk less about you, and more about what you can **do** for your customer. It should ideally call out your ideal customer and say how you help them.

- **Your Job Description**: This is where you focus in detail on who you help, how you help them, what makes you different, the results you deliver, and of course, a call to action for them to contact you.

- **Your Skills and Expertise**: The skills and expertise section is a fantastic way to showcase the solution that you deliver. What's great is that these skills and expertise are searchable by LinkedIn users.

- **Your Comments, Interactions, and Replies**: This is a great way to naturally build rapport with people. The gist is that if you happen to see a great post on LinkedIn, leave a thoughtful, insightful, authentic comment. Share a story, mention what you liked, or simply thank them for writing such a great post. This is a fantastic way to start building a relationship with your prospect.

- **Your Posts**: Publishing posts and videos on LinkedIn is a really good way to engage with your existing audience and connections. Make sure that your posts are helpful, insightful, tell a story, and solve a real problem. Be sure to include story, imagery, and emotion.

- **Your Invite Requests**: Inviting people to connect with you on LinkedIn is a great way to get in touch with new prospects. It's low-risk for them and I usually like to include a friendly, personal note with my invite request. Again, focus on THEM. Mention something about them that caught your eye. This will dramatically improve your chances of getting a response.

- **Your Follow-Up Messages:** Once people have connected with you on LinkedIn, you want to send them personal follow-up messages that continue to talk about them.

Remember, people's **favorite** thing to talk about is themselves. You want to give people that opportunity on LinkedIn. If you can do that, you'll open a whole new world of opportunity.

Like I said earlier, LinkedIn offers so many opportunities to do that. All you have to do is use the tools that LinkedIn has made available.

Niche Down and Scale Up (The Secret to Attracting Your Perfect Customer)

What if I told you that you could 5X your profits by narrowing down your list of prospects?

What if I told you that by repelling, excluding, and ignoring 80% of the market, you could skyrocket your leads and sales?

What if I told you that by hyper-focusing and niching down on a very specific, highly targeted, very small segment of the market, you could make your competition obsolete, while getting more appointments, more leads, and more sales?

Sounds crazy doesn't it? That's exactly what I thought, until I discovered the power of specialization.

One of my mentors, a highly-paid business consultant ran me through an exercise that changed how I saw the market.

He asked me to think of a regular primary care physician, a doctor that sees patients for routine checkups, high blood pressure, the common cold, and other day-to-day ailments that don't require intense, invasive treatments.

Don't get me wrong, being a primary care physician is an honorable and extremely necessary profession. Often times, your primary care physician will make sure that you're healthy year-over-year, and he will let you know if your blood pressure is too high, if you're gaining too much weight, or if you have markers for a host of other ailments that could become really bad over time.

But in terms of income, primary care physicians are some of the hardest working, lowest paid doctors out there. I should know, I worked in healthcare for 10 years and routinely saw how much primary care physicians made. It was often less than $150,000 per year. A respectable salary for sure, but nowhere near the amount of money other doctors make.

Now compare that to a highly-specialized doctor like a surgeon, or a pediatric oncologist, or a reproductive endocrinologist, or an anesthesiologist. Each of these physicians make anywhere from $300,000 to $600,000 per year on average. That's almost twice as much.

The kicker is that they're treating far fewer patients per day. Primary care physicians see up to 25 patients per day. These specialists might see 10, if that.

Of course, being a specialist takes more schooling, and their cases are more complex. But the point is that by specializing in very specific skills, these doctors can make three times as much money as primary care physicians.

What's more is that by focusing on a very specific skill, they build a reputation for themselves and have way less competition. For example, I live in Chicago and if I were to look for a top dermatologist, I'd probably find 10. If I were to look for a top primary care physician, I'd probably get 100 (at least)

That's the power of specialization. More money, less competition, and less time "working" and hustling for new business.

That's what I want for you. I want you to clearly define who you work with, the problems you solve, the industries you serve, and the results you deliver.

And I want you to ignore everyone else.

I know it sounds scary to ignore parts of the market, but think about it like this, by specializing in a very targeted part of your market, you enhance your authority in their eyes. You look more credible. You come across as more of an expert.

For example, let's say you sell office equipment and you're reaching out to companies to sell your products. You could say that you're an office equipment seller and work with companies across the country.

Or you could say that you're an office equipment seller that specializes in healthcare institutions across the East Coast. You focus on the unique needs and challenges of hospitals, clinics, and labs and you understand exactly how important ergonomic, easy-to-clean, lightweight, and durable office furniture is to them.

You could then say that you've worked with dozens, or hundreds of healthcare institutions and you have a deep and intimate knowledge of how multiple doctors work in shared offices, meaning they need compact furniture. You know how nurses work in shared pods and how important it is to have easy to clean furniture that's easy to adjust. You know how patient rooms need larger, wider chairs to accommodate larger and heavier patients.

Can you imagine what would happen if every piece of your marketing material spoke specifically to your target market, their problems, their challenges, their unique needs?

Can you imagine what kind of reputation you would build? Can you imagine how much easier it would be to contact these hospitals if they knew that you only focused on healthcare institutions? What reason would they have to go to Amazon or Office Depot or Staples?

I hope you can see the power of niching down and then scaling up. I know it seems scary to ignore parts of the market, but it's a power move.

By focusing on a target niche, you exude confidence, expertise, authority, and legitimacy.

When you niche down, you become more aware of the problems in your industry. You have a better understanding of the trends. You can speak more intelligently about their problems.

When you do make contact with them, they feel like they're speaking to a specialist, someone that knows exactly what they're going through.

If you try to be everything to everyone, you come across as having low standards and lack of expertise. Like you're just looking to get business from anyone. And that's not a good feeling for a client to feel.

But when you define who you work with** (and who you don't)**, you create a sense of intrigue, mystery, and exclusivity that people naturally want to connect with.

Kind of like approaching people, hoping that it ends up in a relationship. If you approach anyone and everyone you're not likely to get very far. You come across as desperate and having no standards.

But if you exhibit a sense of self-respect, if you communicate that you're looking for a long-term relationship, based on marriage, with a strong, respectful partner, you'll more than likely attract the best, most committed people to you.

So remember this bit of human psychology, to some degree or another, we want what we can't have. If you require someone to qualify themselves to you before interacting with you, they're much more likely to respond.

Believe me when I say that this stuff works.

In fact, a healthcare tech company found me and contacted me on LinkedIn because I said that I do online marketing for health-based software companies.

Just in case you're worried about being "stuck" in a certain industry, **don't worry**. You can always pivot and target a different segment of the market.

Going back to our office equipment retailer, you can always pivot from hospitals to schools and universities, especially on LinkedIn.

You can tweak your profile headline, description, and messaging to fit the market that you're serving.

If you have salespeople working for you, you can have each one of them target a different industry.

So don't feel like you're limiting yourself by targeting a specific niche. Instead, think of it in terms of campaigns. Dedicate a focused amount of time on a specific segment of the market. Get to know them really well. Understand their problems. Create solutions that resonate with them. And then move on to another industry.

Action Item:

I want you to think about who your ideal customer is. Perhaps you already have a buyer persona for who you work with. If so, that's great.

If not, think deeply about the following:

- The problems you solve

- What their problem is _costing_ them

- The consequences of them not solving their problem

- The industries that you're best suited to work with

- The size of company you can best help

- The job titles of your ideal client

- Why they would buy from you (_as opposed to your competitors_)

Those are just some of the questions you need to ask yourself. Craft good answers for them, and make sure that you incorporate them into your LinkedIn profile.

If you're ready, keep reading because this is where the rubber meets the road.

HOW TO CREATE A PROFILE THAT ATTRACTS YOUR PROSPECTS LIKE A MAGNET

In the last chapter I discussed the secret to attracting your ideal client, while simultaneously neutralizing your competition. The secret to doing that is by niching down and staking your claim in a very specific segment of your market.

In this section I'll show you exactly how to do that.

I'm going to discuss how to setup your LinkedIn profile so that it attracts people like a magnet.

It's incredibly easy to do and won't take longer than an hour, **so please take this part seriously**. Because if you do, you'll notice people starting to find you and view your profile before you even start any outreach.

And when that happens, it's very, very fun.

In fact, LinkedIn even notifies you on a weekly basis, telling you how many people have viewed your profile, their job titles, and how they found you.

This is all very, very powerful. And if you have LinkedIn Sales Navigator, you get even more detailed information.

So believe me when I say that it's completely worth it to take this section seriously and follow my instructions.

So I'm going to break down exactly what you need to do, with simple step-by-step instructions.

But before we begin, I want to tell you to update your LinkedIn settings so that your current connections aren't notified of every change that you make. ***This is super important*** because you're going to be making lots of changes over the next days, testing and tweaking what people respond to best. And the last thing you want to do is annoy your current followers and connections.

To disable the profile notification feature just following these instructions:

1) Go to your LinkedIn profile
2) Click "Settings & Privacy"

3)   Look for "Sharing Profile Edits"

4)   Change the selection to "No"

Once you've done that you should be all set. So let's get started.

But remember, this book is meant to be practical, tactical, and actionable, so I'll give you the "quick and dirty" tips to get up and running and start making money with LinkedIn.

And remember, **everything** you do on LinkedIn should be about your target customer

Keep that in mind throughout this chapter.

Step.1: Update Your LinkedIn Profile Picture

Make sure that you have a professional image for your LinkedIn profile picture. You want to be in business attire with a smiling face. Ideally, you should be looking at the camera.

No duck face. No beach vacation pics. No dog pics. Keep it professional and friendly.

Remember, the picture is for your prospects, not you. So give them a profile picture that they would like to see (*professionally of course*)

If you don't currently have a good one, just use your cell phone and take a few and use the best one.

Easy as can be.

Step.2: Update Your LinkedIn Headline

If you know anything about advertising, you'll know that the world's best copywriters spend 80% of their time on the headline of the ad.

Why?

Because their number goal is to grab the reader's attention, gain their interest, and entice them to keep reading, and eventually take action (book a call, download a white paper, purchase a product, click a link, etc.) So the headline for an advertisement is the **most** important part, and because of that, it deserves the most attention.

So when you consider your LinkedIn profile, you have to consider it as an advertisement for you, your business, and your offer.

Now, you only have a limited amount of space for your profile, but if you can, I strongly suggest that you included the following two elements:

Keywords + Target Audience + Benefit Statement (sometimes)

You want to use keywords because these are searchable and they allow prospects to find you on LinkedIn easily.

You want to mention a target audience because they'll instantly feel like you're talking to them (*remember, being everything to everyone is a big no-no*) That intimacy and direct appeal is what will catch their attention.

For example, let's say you're driving down the highway and you see a billboard advertising tires. You've seen hundreds of these in your lifetime, so you ignore it.

Now let's say the billboard says "*Are the tires on your minivan getting worn down from driving your kids to soccer practice everyday? Come in for a free tire assessment*"

If you drive a minivan and cart your kids to activities everyday, this ad is definitely going to get your attention.

Why?

Because they're speaking directly to you. And that creates an emotional response because you feel understood. Remember, niching down creates leverage and emotional intimacy with your prospects. That's exactly what you want.

Here are a few examples that include Keywords + Target Audience + Benefit Statement (sometimes)

Now the reason I say that you should occasionally add a benefit statement is that it could come across as a little spammy. If you lead with how you help people, the prospect may feel on the defensive and sense that you're just trying to pitch them.

"Marketing Strategy | Online Lead Generation | Thought Leadership for SaaS Companies"

Or

"B2B Marketing Strategy | Online Marketing Consulting | Content Marketing for B2B Tech Companies"

Or

"Contract Manufacturing for Consumer Packaged Goods Companies"

Or

"Project Management for Cloud Computing Projects"

Or

"Predictive Analytics | Business Intelligence | SAP HANA for Retail"

Or

"Risk & Strategy Consulting for Oil & Gas"

Or

"Industrial Machinery Supplier for Agribusiness"

Or

"Supply Chain & Logistics for Food and Beverage"

Or

"Learning Management Systems for Training and Development Organizations"

Or

"Executive Coaching for Female C-Suite Execs" (*I really like that one*)

You get the picture.

The point here is that you're using specific keywords that your target market would be searching for on LinkedIn. You're also specifying who you work with, which establishes you as an expert in their industry.

Notice that you aren't talking about yourself, you aren't really mentioning your job title, etc. If you have space, you can enter your job title so they know who you are, but the goal is to show them what you do and who you help.

If you have a title like CEO or Founder or Principal or Managing Director or Partner or VP, I would work those into your headline too because they convey authority. And people are more likely to respond to an authoritative title.

One last method that I've seen work really well is to have a bunch of keywords.

For example:

"Business Coach | Sales Coach | Speaker | Author | Online Engagement Specialist - CEO of Blah Blah Blah Consulting"

Anytime someone says that they're a speaker and author they have instant credibility, so if you're either of those, definitely add them to your headline.

The point is, your marketing becomes much easier when you focus in on a specific segment of the market and focus exclusively on their problems.

Step.3: Update Your LinkedIn Summary:

Your LinkedIn summary is a really valuable piece of real estate on your LinkedIn profile because if you caught your prospects attention, they're more than likely to click and view your profile summary.

You want to write it as a continuation of your LinkedIn "ad". Remember that your headline is designed to get their attention. That's where you say who you help and how you help them.

Your summary is where you continue in that vein and detail who you help, the problems you solve, and the results you deliver. Like any good ad, you want to end it with a strong call to action, directing the reader to contact you.

My favorite way to write a LinkedIn summary, or any sales copy for that matter, is the Problem Agitate Solve (PAS) framework. This is an incredibly powerful copywriting formula used by some of the greatest copywriters in the world.

The reason it's so popular is because it directly addresses the problem that people are facing. And believe me, we're all motivated to avoid pain and solve our problems.

Let's go back to that minivan example I shared earlier where our sample ad called out busy parents whose tire tread is wearing thin because of constant trips to school, activities, and home for their kids. The ad called out a specific audience and mentioned a specific problem that the audience is facing. Doing that causes the ad to jump out to them.

The PAS framework starts off by mentioning a problem that your target customer has.

Whether it's:

- *Struggling to rollout a cloud computing strategy for your hospital imaging system?*

- *Sick of getting low-quality online leads for your construction company?*

- *Low employee engagement causing lost clients at your accounting firm?*

- *Failing industrial equipment causing waste for your farm?*

- *Slow, inefficient supply chains causing customers to buy online rather than visit your store?*

- *Does your clunky learning management system make it hard to measure the effectiveness of your employee training program?*

The point is to address the biggest problems that your industry is facing. To know them well and to understand their root causes. Even if they're not currently facing that problem, you've definitely gotten their attention - because they want to avoid that problem in the future.

Next is to agitate the problem by mentioning the consequences of not solving the problem. This is where you give real-life examples, statistics, and use imagery, emotion, and story.

For example:

- Failing to migrate your data to the cloud means 35% longer patient wait times, 22% lower revenue, and increased data security costs

- Getting low quality online leads from "tire kickers" means you're burning through tens of thousands of dollars per month and losing real deals to your marketing-savvy competitors

- Less engaged employees means more mistakes, less due-diligence, and more angry customers.

- Etc.

The point is to agitate the pain. You want to make it emotional by spelling out the consequences of the problem. You want to remind them of the cost of not solving it.

Marketers call this "*addressing the conversation inside the buyer's head*". And if you want to become good at selling, you HAVE to address that conversation better than anyone else. You have to demonstrate that you know what they're going through, because if you can diagnose their problem, and empathize with what they're going through, you'll dramatically increase your chances of speaking to them and making the sale.

Lastly, you want to offer a solution to the problem. Now that you've demonstrated that you understand their problem and you know the consequences that could happen, you can transition to your solution.

Here are a few examples:

- *Our simple cloud conversion platform makes migrating data from your servers to the cloud quick and easy*

- *Our lead generation service finds you the most qualified leads for your construction projects that are ready to buy*

- *Our employee engagement app helps motivate employees by providing a gamified reward system for project completion milestones*

See what I mean? You're offering a solution in a creative, novel, and simple way. If you did a good job at defining the problem and agitating the consequences, they should be very receptive to the solution.

So let's tie this all together.

Once you've defined who your ideal client is, the problems they have, what it's costing them to not solve them, and how you help them, we'll put it together in a simple format that you can put in your LinkedIn summary section.

Here's what to put in your LinkedIn profile summary:

What We Do:

Mention who you help here in detail. Mention industry, company size, job titles, etc.

This is also where you list the problems that you solve and agitate the problem by mentioning the consequences of not solving them. Get specific and detailed.

Remember, you want to use story, imagery, and emotion to show them that you know what you're talking about and to paint a picture of horror stories you've seen. Doing this enhances your credibility and positions you as an expert and authority.

Results:

The only thing people really care about is results. This is where you talk about your solution, process, service, or product. But remember to focus on the result, the outcome, and the transformation you provide - you're writing for **them** as I said earlier.

Discuss results you've provided for past clients. Use facts, statistics, and figures. People love seeing results. But remember to include a descriptive story about how you turned things around. Like they say, *facts tell, stories sell.*

Contact:

Add your phone number, email, and company website here. You can even mention a free white paper, software demo, or consulting call if you'd like. Think long and hard about what your prospect would want and then offer it to them.

It's really as simple as that.

Step.4: Update the Skills Section

The only other thing that I would do here is to update the skills section of your LinkedIn profile because it includes a lot of keywords that people can find you by.

If you go and start typing you'll see all kinds of skill-based keywords that you can add to your profile. This probably isn't a make or break thing to do, but it's helpful.

Action Items:

So we've covered a lot in this section, but it's relatively simple.

So your action items are to update your LinkedIn picture, headline, and summary. You can tweak your past job experiences but it's not all that necessary.

Your LinkedIn profile is where you want to address your audiences fears, their pain, their needs, their desires… and most of all, how **you** can help them.

So take an hour now to show how you help them and demonstrate your authority.

You'll notice that people will start finding you on LinkedIn and contacting you to help them.

It's incredibly powerful.

I'm speaking from experience because I've had people find my profile on LinkedIn, contact me, and buy from me - all within a few days of me updating my profile like I showed you above.

HOW TO INSTANTLY FIND YOUR IDEAL CLIENTS ON LINKEDIN

Now that you've got a profile that focuses on how you help your prospects, you want to start finding them on LinkedIn.

Luckily, LinkedIn makes this extremely easy.

To find your ideal clients on LinkedIn, we're just going to use the LinkedIn search feature. The key is to be really clear on who you help. That way you can refine your search parameters around your ideal client.

I've said this before, but I want you to think deeply about who your work with, the problems you solve, the consequences of those problems, and lastly how you can help solve that problem.

If you're still worried that limiting yourself to a specific segment of the market, keep in mind that when you get really clear on who you serve, it's **much** easier to actually find them.

It's kind of like going to a food court in the mall. You know you're hungry and there are 20+ restaurants, so it can be overwhelming. But if you define from the start that you want to eat something healthy (*not deep fried fast food*), it instantly makes it easier to decide where to eat.

Here's another example, if you want to sell your SaaS marketing software, selling to everyone and everyone is taxing and overwhelming. However, limiting yourself to construction companies, it becomes a whole lot easier to find those companies and to position yourself to actually help them.

The last story I want to share about defining a target market is about the mega-popular online accounting software FreshBooks.com

Freshbooks has grown to over 4.5 million users using a niche growth strategy like I'm talking about and then "island hopping" to other industries.

"Island hopping" was the military strategy the U.S. used in World War II to take over island after island from the Japanese in the Pacific Ocean. They would focus their efforts on a Japanese controlled island, take it over, and then hop over to the next island.

So FreshBooks decided to use a similar strategy.

They created a list of all different verticals and professions that *could* use them, then decided to focus on one at a time.

They first focused on creative professionals that live and work on their computers (graphic designers, web developers, etc.)

Then they moved on to other professions and industries.

So if the idea of honing in on a niche market scares you because you feel like you're limiting yourself and closing yourself off from other opportunities, **don't**.

View yourself as "*island hopping*" from industry to industry.

The beauty of this strategy is that as you accumulate more customers, you'll have more case studies that you can reference. You can mention how your current focus is XYZ industry, but that you've successfully solved this same problem in other industries.

So I hope you understand the power of targeting a specific market. It amplifies your messaging, makes it easier to find prospects, and establishes you as an authority.

Ok, now to the meat and potatoes of searching for your target market on LinkedIn. There are a few different parameters you're going to use to find your ideal prospect, but it's all done in the LinkedIn search bar.

As far as finding people, there are a few main strategies:

You can search for people by job title...

You can search by viewing members of groups and associations you're part of...

You can search by interest and affiliation...

How to Search for People by Job Title in the LinkedIn Search Bar

This is relatively straightforward, you simply type in the job title of your ideal customer, choose a connection level, and possibly a geographic region, industry, or company size.

So if I wanted to look for directors of security for hospitals, I would do this:

1) Go to the LinkedIn search bar and choose "People"

2) Enter the job title I'm looking for, in this case, I'll enter "Director of Security"

3) Click "All Filters" to expand your search criteria

4) Enter the following search criteria:

   - **Connections:** 2nd Level (this lets me search connections of my existing connections)

   - **Locations:** United States (or maybe a geographic region of the US if you only focus on a certain territory)

   - **Industries:** Type in the industry/industries that you're targeting (in this case "Hospitals & Health Care")

5) Then I'd hit "Apply"

When I do this, it gives me a list of over 2,100 people.

Jackpot!

[*Now, you need to treat this list of people with extreme care and respect. This is* NOT *a license to spam them.*

In the next section, I'm going to share a simple strategy to message them based on relationship building and creating a personal connection, NOT *selling.*]

What's even cooler is the "OR" and "AND" and "NOT" search feature.

Let's say you want to look for a director of IT that does not work for Dell. You'd enter:

"Director of IT" NOT "Dell"

And that will give you a list of directors of IT for companies that do not include Dell.

Or let's say you're looking for two types of job titles like VP of Engineering and VP of Technology. In that case, you'd enter:

"Vice President of Technology" OR "VP of Technology" OR "Vice President of Engineering" OR "VP of Engineering"

Or let's say you're looking for Chief Operating Officers for healthcare companies. You'd enter:

"COO" AND "Healthcare"

Pretty cool, huh?

If you know who you want to target, LinkedIn makes it extremely easy to find them.

Keep in mind, you can do this with a free LinkedIn account, but purchasing a Sales Navigator account makes this much easier because you can search with even more granularity and you can create lead lists in LinkedIn that you can go back to.

With Sales Navigator, you also get to see how active your prospects are on LinkedIn.

Ideally, you want to work with people that have been active on LinkedIn in the past 30 days.

On top of that, you can also send InMail's, which is LinkedIn's high priority messaging system.

That said, a Sales Navigator account is pricey. I've found their $79.99/month option to be the most useful because it gives the following benefits:

- Ability to send 20 InMail messages per month

- Insights on news and job changes for your leads

- Advanced search function

- Who's viewed your profile

- Unlimited search and browsing

- Ability to create lead lists

Again, it's not necessary to use the paid plan, but if you're going to spend a significant amount of time on LinkedIn, you may consider using it.

Best of all, LinkedIn offers a free 30-day trial, so take it for a spin and cancel if you don't like it.

Action Items:

Take the time to perform a few searches on LinkedIn.

Search based on job title, industry, company size, geography, etc.

Be sure to search "2nd" or "3rd" contacts, that way you're searching for friends of your friends or complete strangers. If you just search your current 1st-level contacts, you won't turn up many prospects.

If you want even more functionality, you can subscribe to LinkedIn Premium and see how you like it. I do think it's valuable if you plan on using LinkedIn a lot.

THE MIND-BLOWING LINKEDIN NETWORKING STRATEGY

This is an exciting chapter for me and you.

It's exciting for you because you're going to see the best way to use LinkedIn to contact potential clients, build a relationship with them, and ultimately work with them.

It's exciting for me because this is stuff that most people don't know - and it's exciting for me to share how to use LinkedIn properly.

Because I'm going to share a little secret with you. It's a secret known by some of the most successful people in the world.

Professional athletes.

World-class chefs.

Sex therapists.

Multi-millionaire real estate developers.

Want to know the secret?

It's simple.

They all know that they can't rush straight into their craft. **That's it**.

Athletes need to *warm up* before a big game.

Chefs need to *preheat an oven* and prep their ingredients before they create an incredible meal.

Sex therapists teach their clients that *foreplay* is critical to a great romantic experience.

Real estate developers understand the importance of *building a strong foundation* before constructing a massive building.

The key here is that before you do anything on LinkedIn, you've got to do your prep work. You've got to lay a foundation. You've got to take the time to start things off **_right_** before you ever start selling.

Most people completely *screw this up*.

They're quick to talk about *themselves*.

They try to *sell right away*.

They send *cold, impersonal* messages *that they cut and paste* over and over again.

All of this has made prospects on LinkedIn incredibly jaded, suspicious, and unresponsive.

That's why so many people feel like their LinkedIn message box is a cesspool of sleazy sales pitches and scammy offers.

But you're going to do things differently.

You're going to focus on building a relationship. You're going to learn about your prospect. You're going to talk less about you and more about them. You're going to find something in common between you and them and use that to introduce yourself.

Keep in mind that LinkedIn provides a wealth of information about your prospects, and it's basically handed to you on a silver platter.

Think about it like this… on LinkedIn, you have a wealth of information at your fingertips. Information that you can use to get to know your prospects on a deeper, more intimate level.

You get to see what school your prospect went to and when they graduated.

You get to see where they've worked in the past.

You see what fraternities, sororities, professional organizations, and civic groups they're part of.

You get to see their interests, hobbies, and birthday, and marital status.

That's a LOT of information at your disposal.

So when you reach out to do business with someone on LinkedIn, why wouldn't you reference that information?

Why wouldn't you start with something you have in common, like a common school, or working at the same company in the past, or being part of the same organization, or that they share similar hobbies as you?

Even if you don't have anything in common with them, you surely can find something interesting about them, can't you?

You can reference that in your message to them, you can use that to start a conversation and build a relationship.

Do you see where I'm going with this? Can you see how powerful LinkedIn is? Can you see how you can use all of this information to make yourself unique, authentic, and personable?

I sure hope so.

And don't worry, even if prospects ignore your messages on LinkedIn, you should have multiple touch points by which you can contact them because you know so much about them.

So let's get started.

Step.1: Look at Their Profile

Now that you have a list of contacts (see the previous chapter), I want you to invest time to get to know them.

That means you need to read their profile.

You need to check out their website.

You need to look at what school they went to, what organizations they're a part of, what interests they have, and what career goals they've shared.

The point is that you want to understand what's important to them before you ever think of reaching out.

71

Step.2: Read, Like, Comment, and Share Their Content

If your prospect has written a post or commented on LinkedIn, they'll have a section on their profile called "Activity".

The "Activity" section will show posts and articles that they've written on Linked, but it will also show posts and articles that they've liked and commented on.

This is amazing because you get to see not only what they write, but what they like.

Note: One of the best ways to get on someone's radar is to like, comment, and share their content - especially if they've been active on LinkedIn in the past 30 days.

People love attention. They love being validated. They love being recognized. They love feeling like their work has made an impact.

If you simply like, comment, and share posts that others have written, you'll get their attention because LinkedIn notifies them that you've liked their content.

Even if they haven't written any of their own content but have commented on **other** people's content, you can reply to their comment.

You can simply say how much you liked their post and how you agree with the point that they're making.

This strategy is incredibly powerful for getting people's attention and is used by some of the world's best marketers.

Believe it or not, I've spent hundreds of dollars to learn this simple little tip.

And I'm glad I did because I've tried emailing people directly and asking them for something and either got ignored, or they would flatly say "no".

On the other hand, I've gotten meetings with very high-level people by simply liking their content, leaving an intelligent comment referencing something that I read or liked, and then shared it.

If you want to go even further, you can tag them when you share their content to make sure they know that you appreciate their work.

(Tagging someone is very easy on LinkedIn, all you do is use @ and enter their name)

Oftentimes, this strategy alone is enough to start a conversation with a key decision maker on LinkedIn.

You definitely want to use it.

In fact, 7-figure entrepreneur Vanessa van Edwards shared how she launched her best-selling book by contacting influencers 18-months before she released her own book.

She went on to say that she make a spreadsheet of the launches of influential people that _**she**_ admired. Then, 6-weeks before they launched, she contacted them asking if she could help promote their product.

As you can imagine, they all enthusiastically said "yes".

Then, when it came time for her to launch her book, she was able to reach out to them and they were more than happy to help.

You want to use the same principle.

Like, comment, and share your prospects content before you contact them. That way, when you eventually do, they're primed to engage with you.

Step.3: Send a Friendly Invite Request

Hopefully, by now you've liked and commented on their content (whether it's their own original content or a comment that they left on someone else's post).

If you have, they most likely know about you now.

The next step is to send them a friendly connection request.

Now, this is critical because you only have one shot to connect with them.

So I highly suggest that you send them a friendly, personal message that references something about **them** (as opposed to you, your company, or your offer)

You can mention a piece of content of theirs that you liked.

Or the fact that you went to the same school.

Or a shared organization that you belong to.

It doesn't matter what you lead with as long as your message demonstrates that you've done your homework and are genuinely interested in them.

Here's an example of a connection request you can send:

"Hi Sarah,

I just read your LinkedIn post on the state of healthcare and thought you made some great points. I noticed that you've worked in healthcare for the past 10 years - so cool!

I'd love to connect if you're open to it.

Raza"

It's simple, direct, slightly flattering, and shows that I've done my homework.

Don't underestimate the power of that simple connection request.

Your goal is to send 10-20 of these per day.

But remember, you have to do the groundwork first. That means looking at their profile, commenting on their content, sharing it, etc.

Then when you reach out to them you've already built up some goodwill.

This is why the previous step of liking, commenting, and sharing their content is so critical.

Remember the story of Vanessa van Edwards I referenced above? She said that one of her secrets to contacting people was to become known to them <u>before</u> she actually contacted them.

It makes life so much easier when you do the groundwork.

Step.4: Send Another Personal Message Once They Respond

Now that you're on your prospects radar, and assuming they've responded to your connection request, you can build the relationship further.

But remember, it's much better to interact with them publicly, via comments on their content, because they're more likely to respond to you.

Once you've established a relationship with them, and they've publicly acknowledged and replied to your comments, you can get more personal with them via LinkedIn Messenger.

Now what most people do is go "straight for the kill" and make a sales pitch.

But if you remember my discussion of foreplay, preheating, and warming up, diving straight into a sales pitch is the **wrong** approach.

Instead, you want to figure out how you can help them.

Now, a super secret method to do that is to use the LinkedIn voice note feature to send them an audio message.

If done correctly, this is *gold*. It helps them see you as a real person.

The key is for you to make your message friendly and personable.

Again, mention something that you noticed about them. Mention something that you have in common. And then casually mention something that you can help them with.

You can say something like this:

"Hey Sarah, thanks so much for connecting.

Your profile jumped out at me because _____. *I've worked with companies like yours in the past, so I was really intrigued by the work you're doing at* _____.

I did some research and wanted to run an idea by you that I thought would be helpful and was wondering if you're open to me sharing it."

See how straight forward that is?

In most cases, if the person is active on LinkedIn, they'll respond with a resounding "yes".

Why?

Because you were polite, created intrigue, and asked permission.

These simple messages work like gang-busters, here's why:

- **Courtesy**: These messages are courteous and thankful

- **Establish Authority**: They reference work that I'm currently doing

- **Research**: They show that I've done my homework and am genuinely interested in what they're doing

- **Expertise**: They demonstrate that I have an idea of value that could help _**them**_

- **Permission**: They ask permission and are humble (don't underestimate the power of asking permission)

- **Curiosity**: They create intrigue, curiosity, and mystery. And curiosity is one of the most powerful triggers of action.

Remember, the key is to be kind, courteous, humble, friendly, unique, and mysterious.

I'm not talking about trying to attract the opposite sex, but I might as well be!

The reason is that humans are humans and we all want to be treated with respect and kindness.

But we also respond much better to mystery, intrigue, and curiosity than we do to outright, direct, blatant requests.

We also take notice of people that are different, unique, one-of-a-kind, and novel.

That's the power of the message strategy I shared above.

Now if you want to make this even more powerful, you can send them a video response.

I use Screencastify.com to create short videos from my computer screen. If you want to use your phone, you can create a video on your phone and share it that way.

The bottom line is that creating personal, authentic, genuine messages that actually help them is the #1 way to get your prospects to respond to you.

Once they respond to you, you can talk about how you can schedule a call, demo, webinar, etc.

Believe me, if you follow this process, and invest at least an hour per day, or a few hours every other day, you'll see great results.

Bonus: "*What If This Doesn't Work?*"

The strategy I shared above works amazingly well, if you follow it properly.

But, if it doesn't, you still will have made an impression on your prospect. And if they check LinkedIn at all, they will have seen all of the engagement you've done with their content, the mentions you've made about them, etc.

The next step is to simply email them.

If they accepted your LinkedIn invite but haven't responded to your messages, you can simply look up their email address in their LinkedIn profile. That's another data point that LinkedIn has (*in addition to past employment, schools, interests, groups, professional organizations, hobbies, and birthday!*)

In fact, emailing people **_after_** you've engaged with them and mentioned them on LinkedIn might be an even better strategy than messaging them on LinkedIn.

Why?

The LinkedIn message box has become a cesspool.

As soon as you accept an invite from someone, they'll usually start pitching you.

That's why most people will accept LinkedIn invites, but won't really engage in the LinkedIn message box.

Well, there are a few online copywriters named Charlie Price and Alex Berman. These young guys have built advertising agencies that make $1 million per year (if I recall correctly) and they've built their business using LinkedIn and cold emailing their prospects - these guys are in their 20's!

Alex Berman says that he prefers email because decision makers **always** check their email. Early in the morning, at night, on weekends - all the time.

Some of them exclusively read and send emails all day long. Multi-millionaire SaaS entrepreneur and investor Jason Lemkin was asked if cold email still works and he mentioned this very fact on an answer on Quora - that cold emailing executives works if your message is on point and adds value.

Just imagine how much more effective this strategy would be if you did all of that work to "warm" them up on LinkedIn.

Another way to get on their radar is to retweet a piece of content of theirs. Or comment on their blog. Or leave a review on their podcast.

With each one these actions, you're making a deposit in their emotional bank account. You're sharing their content, you're leaving reviews on their podcast, you're commenting on their blog.

All of this will make you stand out from your competitors.

Believe me when I say; ***this stuff works***.

All you have to do is do the work.

Action Items:

This chapter is one of the most powerful chapters in this entire book because it shows you exactly how to get noticed by your prospects before you ever contact them. Then, once you're on their radar, you connect with them in a friendly, authentic manner. Then you build a relationship with them.

- Search for people in your target market (get as specific as possible)

- Send 10 **personal** invites per day (mention something you noticed about them)

- When they respond, send them an audio and text message that mentions what you thought was so cool about them

- Make a post on LinkedIn about something cool that you noticed about them, be authentic and sincere (remember, this is about THEM, **not** you)

As an action item, you want to spend at least 30 minutes per day connecting with 10 prospects doing the following:

1) Look at your target market's profiles

2) Read, like, comment, and reply to their content and comments

3) Send a friendly invite request

4) Send a personal message after they accept your request (use an audio note or video)

5) See if you can help them in their business somehow

6) Continue to like, reply, and comment on their content on LinkedIn

7) Send a friendly, personal email to them mentioning that you noticed them on LinkedIn and wanted to share an idea with them

Schedule it and put it in your calendar. Get used to the process of spending at least 30 minutes per day and contacting 10 people.

You may only get a 30% to 40% response rate, so staying consistent will keep you motivated and focused. Focus on the system, the process, and the task at hand rather than the end result.

That's how you keep making progress.

EXTRA LINKEDIN TIPS

Like I said at the beginning of this book, I want to keep this short and sweet.

You know, the whole "*I'm busy, you're busy…*" thing.

The goal is to give you the **hardest hitting**, **most impactful**, **most actionable advice** I possibly can in this book.

There are a few more odds and ends that I wanted to include in this chapter. It's all helpful, but I don't think they warrant a chapter of their own.

1). Mention Your Connections in a Post

A great strategy to increase engagement and the chance that your new prospects will respond to you is to tag everyone that connected with you this week.

This is an amazing way to get lots of eyeballs to your post (and subsequently your LinkedIn profile) because people will like, comment, and share your post, causing their connections to see it.

You can do the same thing with your existing contacts. Just do a post that mentions something cool about them.

By tagging multiple people in a single post, you're seen as a connector and influencer.

Here's an example of a post I wrote:

"Here are some awesome people I've (re)connected with over the past week.

Check out the cool stuff they're doing...

J Schwan congrats on being featured as one of the fastest growing tech firms in Chicago - you guys are ballers!

Elvin Rakhmankulov is a mobile app architecture expert

Luis A. Márquez is a cutting-edge digital strategist

Sebastian Vazquez is helping companies manage their HR functions with their cloud-based solution

Sibu Kutty is an expert enterprise cloud architect

Lindsay R. Hall helps commercial real estate firms manage their telecom infrastructure

Steve Susina is helping dentists grow their practices

Joe Piekarz is making the painful task of time tracking MUCH easier

John Head is helping big companies collaborate better

Emile Cambry is a genius that's creating a really cool tech + entrepreneurship incubator

David Carman is creating Chicago's premier fin-tech hub

Aasil Ahmad runs a cutting-edge marketing start-up that's going to change how companies speak to their customers

Ron Kirschner is a veteran business leader turned professor

Allan Cox helps Fortune 500 execs perform at their best

Timothy Kelley is one of the top medical imaging providers in the country

These guys and gals are amazing so don't forget to like, share, and comment!"

Mentioning people that you've recently connected with is a great way to get tons of exposure (because they'll like, share, and comment on your post).

It also builds a lot of goodwill with them, making it easier to contact them and build a relationship.

2). Record Live Videos

Video is **hot** these days.

Facebook, Instagram, and of course YouTube are investing heavily in their video platforms.

And so is LinkedIn.

Some sources say that LinkedIn gives preferential treatment to video in their algorithm, meaning you'll be more views on your video than if you created a text post.

Telling stories, sharing solutions to problems, and showcasing clients are all great video ideas.

Remember, by sharing your own videos on LinkedIn, you're strengthening the bond with your existing connections on LinkedIn. That way you're staying relevant to people that may not have needed your help in the past.

Honestly, some of the most engaging videos that I've seen on LinkedIn have been shot on a cell phone.

People don't care about production quality, they don't care about what you look like, they care about how you can help them.

If you can tell a story, with imagery and emotion, and paint a picture of what their future could look like, they'll reach out to you when they have a need for what you offer.

Creating videos is a particularly good way to stay engaged with your LinkedIn connections that don't currently need your product or service.

But if you record a short 2-5 minute video every week, they'll be sure to contact you when the time comes.

3). Write Articles on LinkedIn

You may already know that LinkedIn has a publishing platform.

Anytime you create a new piece of content on your blog, you should also publish it on LinkedIn.

5-10 years ago, search engine optimization experts would publish articles on large websites like EzineArticles.com, Weebly.com, Squidoo.com, and other huge websites that allow user-generated content.

At the end of each article, they'd leave a link to their website or an affiliate product that they received a commission for.

Some of these people didn't even bother to create their own website. They simply "borrowed" the authority of these large websites to have their articles rank highly in Google.

The idea is that Google trusts larger, more authoritative sites, so they would publish articles on these sites and have them rank highly.

It was called "article marketing" and it was a pretty smart strategy - because it **worked**.

You want to do the same on LinkedIn.

Not because you'll get a lot of traffic from people on LinkedIn, but because if you perform proper keyword research, and choose medium competition keywords, your article can rank well on Google.

Be sure to include a call to action at the end of the article that links back to your website.

Personal development articles and videos do really well. Just look at Inc, Business Insider, and the Ladders

If you really want to make an impression on a prospect, you could do an entire article on them and publish it on LinkedIn. Be sure to tag them in the article.

I did this for a company that I was targeting once and got massive amounts of views and likes.

4). Automation

LinkedIn does not like automated tools that mimic human behavior.

So keep that in mind.

That said, many people are doing very well using automation on LinkedIn.

They send out 25-100 invites per day.

Then they send personal replies via LinkedIn Messenger to people that accept the connection request.

If anyone replies to those messages, they'll engage in a real conversation.

I don't personally do this because if LinkedIn catches you, they'll issue you a warning. If you keep doing it, they'll ban your account.

However, I know of people that are doing quite well on LinkedIn using automated tools.

The most popular and powerful tool on the market these days is MeetLeonard. I've tried multiple tools but this is the easiest to use and has the lightest footprint.

My friend John Nemo has an entire video (*which I wholeheartedly vouch for*) that shows you how to set up automation and thrive.

5). Focus on Active Members

When you start out on LinkedIn, you'll get the best results by focusing on people that have been active on LinkedIn in the past 90 days.

If they haven't, that's ok, because I already shared how you can mention them on Twitter, via email, leave a comment on their company blog, write a post about them on LinkedIn, etc.

But focusing on people that are active on LinkedIn makes it a lot easier.

Note: You can only see how active they are with a paid Sales Navigator account.

CASE STUDIES

We're almost at the end of this book, so I wanted to leave you with a few case studies to build up your belief, excitement, and motivation.

Take a look at these case studies and then put LinkedIn into action!

1). My Story

Like I said at the beginning of this book, I used to think LinkedIn was a waste of time for business.

But then I saw other people around me finding jobs and getting business on LinkedIn, so I decided to double down, invest in learning how to use it, and take action.

Shortly after updating my LinkedIn profile (like I showed you earlier), a friend of mine contacted me to help him with content marketing.

Not long after that, the CEO of a healthcare tech company contacted me to help with his website copy and content marketing.

All in all, I made $20,000 in roughly 2 months, just by using the strategies I share in this book.

2). John Nemo

I've mentioned my friend and mentor John Nemo before, but here's his story.

John used to work in corporate America, but after learning how to use LinkedIn, he quit his job and started getting clients.

Within 90 days, he had acquired $120,000 of business - all on LinkedIn!

How?

He had experience with debt collection agencies, so he decided to focus on doing marketing for debt collection agencies.

By defining a niche and focusing in on it, he really differentiated himself from his competitors.

Rather than selling generic marketing services, he focused his entire messaging and positioning around marketing for debt collection agencies - and profited handsomely from it.

3). Bill Prater

Bill Prater is a business strategy consultant that built his business by meeting business owners in person.

He didn't have much experience with marketing online so he took the time to learn how to use LinkedIn.

In just a short time, he was having meetings with companies that he had met on LinkedIn.

And if I recall correctly, he even closed a $90,000 deal from a business owner he met on LinkedIn.

Now he regularly invests a few afternoons a week actively reaching out to his target market on LinkedIn.

4). Benjamin Tyler

Benjamin Tyler is a marketing coach that helps financial advisors grow their client base.

By niching down, he's able to differentiate himself and his services by focusing exclusively on his target market.

Last I heard, he was doing really well.

5). Mohammad F.

My good friend Mohammad has a business intelligence technology consulting company.

He used LinkedIn to find a larger company that wanted to outsource some of their BI tech work to a smaller company like his.

CONCLUSION

Hopefully, you see the power of LinkedIn and are starting to see the world of opportunity that awaits you.

If you take it seriously, invest the time to build relationships, and remain committed to the process, you can also get amazing results.

I wanted this book to give you the simple duplicatable secrets to making a lot of money with LinkedIn.

If you take this seriously, follow the steps I reveal, and create a system to research, connect with, and engage with your prospects, you'll do quite well.

Best of luck and feel free to contact me if you have any questions!

Awesome Recommended Resources

Here's a list of recommended resources for LinkedIn that I've personally gone through.

1) Free LinkedInRiches Training Webinar - www.JaggedEdgeDigital.com/LinkedInRiches

2) LinkedIn Automation Software - www.JaggedEdgeDigital.com/MeetLeonard

If you have any questions about these, just email me at raza.imam@jaggededgedigital.com and I'll answer them to the best of my ability.

Free Training Video

Thank you for buying LinkedIn Sales Machine. If you follow the advice in this book, you'll get amazing results.

If you want a free training webinar that walks you through the entire process, provides live examples, and shares real-life results, then go to:

www.JaggedEdgeDigital.com/LinkedInRiches

It's a brief webinar by my friend and mentor John Nemo that walks through the entire process of marketing on LinkedIn. I've watched it multiple times and learned a ton from it.

More Help

If you're interested in:

- More advice

- A done-for-you marketing service

- Training for you and your team

email me at raza.imam@jaggededgedigital.com to discuss how we can work together.

Before You Leave
a Review...

Thank you again for buying and reading this book. If you got this far, it's because you finished the book, so congratulations!

Authors live and die by the reviews we receive from our readers. So if you liked this book, I'd really appreciate if you left it a 5-star review.

If you didn't like this book, <u>before you leave a negative review</u>, please email me at <u>raza.imam@jaggededgedigital.com</u> and let me know what you would like me to improve. The beauty of publishing online is that I can instantly add content, fix errors, and update information.

So if there's something you didn't like, or that you'd like me to remove, please email me so I can fix it.

Thanks!

Made in the USA
Middletown, DE
12 April 2019